Mollusks

Ruth Miller

Raintree

Chicago, Illinois

© 2005 Raintree
Published by Raintree, a division of Reed Elsevier Inc.
Chicago, Illinois
Customer Service 888-363-4266
Visit our website at www.raintreelibrary.com

For information, address the publisher:
Raintree, 100 N. LaSalle, Suite 1200, Chicago, IL 60602

Produced for Raintree by
White-Thomson Publishing Ltd.

Consultant: Dr. Rod Preston-Mafham
Page layout by Tim Mayer
Photo research by Morgan Interactive Ltd.

Originated by Dot Gradations Ltd.
Printed in China by WKT Company Limited

09 08 07 06 05
10 9 8 7 6 5 4 3 2 1

Library of Congress Cataloging-in-Publication Data
Miller, Ruth, 1936-
    Mollusks / Ruth Miller.
        p. cm. -- (Animal kingdom)
    Includes bibliographical references (p.   ) and index.
    Contents: Mollusk life cycle -- Mollusk classification --
Gastropods -- Land gastropods -- Bivalves -- The giant clam --
The
octopus -- Disappearing mollusks -- Conserving mollusks.
    ISBN 1-4109-1051-2 (lib. bdg : hardcover) -- ISBN 1-4109-
1347-3 (pbk.)
    1. Mollusks--Juvenile literature. [1. Mollusks.] I. Title. II.
Series: Animal kingdom (Chicago, Ill.)
    QL405.2.M56 2004
    594--dc22

                                    i 2003026319

Acknowledgments
The publisher would like to thank the following for permission
to reproduce copyright materials : Corbis pp. **8**, **13**, **15** bottom,
24 bottom (Brandon Cole), **30**, **48**; Digital Vision **Title**,
Contents (main), pp. **4**, **5** background, **21** bottom, **42**, **44**
bottom, **45**; Ecoscene **Contents** left and right (Jeff Collett), pp. **6**
(John Lewis), **9** bottom (Kjell Sandved), **10** (John Lewis), **11**
bottom (Kevin King), **18** (Reinhard Dirscherl), **22**, **23** (Kjell
Sandved), **26**, **27** bottom (Jeff Collett), **29** top (Reinhard
Dirscherl), **31** left (John Lewis), **32** (Reinhard Dirscherl), **38-39**
Jeff Collett, **39** top (Alan Towse), **40** (John Liddiard), **43** (Kevin
King), **44** top (Frank Blackburn); Ecoscene-Papilio pp. **5** top,
15, **34** (Robert Pickett); Nature Photo Library pp. **9** top (Jason
Smalley), **12** top (Jeff Foott), **27** top (Georgette Douwma),
NHPA pp. **7** top (Paal Hermansen), **7** bottom (Linda Pitkin), **12**
(Norbert Wu), **14** (Stephen Dalton), **16** (Roy Waller), **17** right
(Matt Bain), **17** left (Laurie Campbell), **19** top (Patrick O'Neill),
19 bottom (B Jones and M Shimlock), **20** (Robert Thompson),
21 top (Stephen Dalton), **23** top (B Jones and M Shimlock), **23**
bottom (G Bernard), **24** top (Trevor McDonald), **25** top (Roy
Waller), **28** top (B Jones and M Shimlock), **31** right (ANT), **33**
top (Bill Wood), **33** bottom (B Jones and M Shimlock), **35**
bottom (Daniel Heuclin), **36** right (G Bernard), **39** bottom (Roy
Waller), **41** top (G Bernard), **41** bottom (Nigel Callow);
Photodisc pp. **5** bottom, **11** top, **28-29**, **35** top, **46**; Patrick
Reynolds p. **37**.

Front cover photograph of snails reproduced with permission of
Corbis (Anthony Bannister/ Gallo). Back cover image of a snail is
reproduced with permission of Getty Images.

Every effort has been made to contact copyright holders of any
material reproduced in this book. Any omissions will be rectified
in subsequent printings if notice is given to the publisher.

Contents

Introducing Mollusks

Mollusks form a large phylum of invertebrate animals—the second largest group after arthropods. There are about 100,000 known mollusk species found in a wide variety of marine, freshwater, and land habitats.

There are seven classes of mollusks. The three main classes are bivalves, gastropods, and cephalopods. Cephalopods are found only in the sea, but gastropods and bivalves live in marine and freshwater habitats. Some gastropods, such as slugs and garden snails, have adapted to live on land and cannot live in water. The aplacophorans, monoplacophorans, scaphopods, and polyplacophorans form the minor classes.

► More than three quarters of mollusks are gastropods. The soft body and prominent tentacles of this slug are characteristic mollusk features.

Appearance

Mollusks differ greatly in appearance, although they do share a basic body plan. Most mollusks have a well-developed head, with tentacles and eyes. The head is usually joined to a flat, muscular foot. Above the foot, the body organs are contained in a hump covered by a sheet of tissue called the mantle. There is also a space, called the mantle cavity, between the mantle and the rest of the body. This has a different purpose in different types of mollusks.

Classification key

KINGDOM	Animalia
PHYLUM	**Mollusca**
CLASSES	7 – Aplacophora (worm-shaped solenogasters and deep-sea wormlike Caudofoveata), Polyplacophora (chitons), Monoplacophora, Bivalvia (cockles, clams, and mussels), Scaphopoda (tusk shells), Gastropoda (snails and slugs), Cephalopoda (octopuses, cuttlefish, squid, and nautiluses)
ORDERS	35
FAMILIES	about 232
SPECIES	over 100,000

Aquatic mollusks, such as the edible mussel, have gills in their mantle cavities. In land mollusks, the cavity forms a lung. In mollusks that have shells, the mantle produces the materials that make the shell.

Some mollusks, such as bivalves, are filter feeders that get their food from the water in which they live. They use their gills to trap tiny organisms. Many gastropods and cephalopods have a rough, tonguelike structure in the mouth. This structure is covered with rows of tiny, sharp teeth that are used to scrape particles of food into the mouth.

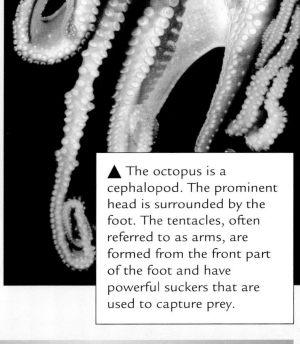

The head has well-developed tentacles and eyes.

A hard shell surrounds the hump containing body organs.

The flat, muscular foot allows the mollusk to move around.

▲ The octopus is a cephalopod. The prominent head is surrounded by the foot. The tentacles, often referred to as arms, are formed from the front part of the foot and have powerful suckers that are used to capture prey.

▲ The snail is a land gastropod.

Classification

Living organisms are classified, or organized, according to how closely related one organism is to another. The basic group in classification is the species. For example, human beings belong to the species *Homo sapiens*. A species is a group of individuals that are similar to each other and can interbreed with one another. Species are grouped together into genera (singular: genus). A genus may contain a number of species that share some features. *Homo* is the human genus. Genera are grouped together in families; families grouped into orders; and orders grouped into classes. Classes are grouped together in phyla (singular: phylum) and finally, the phyla are grouped into kingdoms. Kingdoms are the largest groups. Mollusks belong to the phylum Mollusca in the animal kingdom.

Mollusk Life Cycle and Behavior

Mollusks have a wide variety of body forms. In most mollusks, the egg hatches into a larva, an early stage of development between fertilized egg and adult. Aquatic mollusks have free-swimming larvae. In some aquatic species, the egg hatches into a simple larva that is covered in tiny hairs, or cilia. This is called a trochophore larva. This stage quickly develops into a more complex veliger larva, which has many adult features including a head, a foot, and a tiny shell. In other species, this development takes place inside the egg and the veliger larva emerges on hatching. In land mollusks such as snails and in cephalopods such as octopuses, all the larval stages take place within the egg before hatching.

Males and females

Some mollusks, such as snails, are hermaphrodites. This means that individuals have both male and female sex organs. Others, such as mussels and cephalopods, have separate sexes. Some bivalves and gastropods can change sex during their lifetimes. For example, oysters are bivalves that may mature as males before becoming female and producing eggs. After the eggs have been released, the oyster becomes a male again.

▼ There are no larval stages in the life cycle of the cuttlefish, so the young hatch as miniature adults. Even when young, the eyes are very prominent.

The garden snail

The common garden snail, *Helix aspersa*, is a hermaphrodite gastropod. In this species, mating results in the exchange of male sex cells between partners. Two snails circle each other, touching each other with their tentacles, before becoming entwined. The sex cells are then exchanged and stored inside each snail's body until the eggs are laid a few weeks later. The eggs are usually laid in damp soil in small batches of about 50. Each tough shell contains a yolk. Inside the eggs, the larval stages develop and the eggs grow bigger. After a week or two, the young snails hatch.

Amazing facts

- The courtship of the great gray slug can last for more than an hour. Two slugs circle each other, producing large amounts of mucus. They crawl up a wall or tree trunk and mate in mid-air at the end of a string of sticky mucus.
- A female octopus can lay 150,000 eggs in a week.

▲ When slugs such as these black slugs mate, they twist around each other and produce large quantities of sticky mucus.

Cephalopod life cycles

Cuttlefish are a group of cephalopods in which the sexes are separate. After courtship, mating occurs. The female's eggs are laid singly, each attached to seaweed or coral by a thread. Miniature cuttlefish hatch from these fertilized eggs.

After a female octopus has laid her eggs, she looks after them for several weeks. She keeps them clean with her arms and blows water over them. During the time she spends looking after the eggs, she does not eat and may die soon afterward.

◄ During courtship, the male cuttlefish develops a striped pattern on his body and swims above the female before depositing a sac of sperm into her mantle cavity.

Feeding Methods

Mollusks have a wide range of feeding methods. There are carnivores, herbivores, and omnivores. Some mollusks are parasites, which means they feed on host animals without killing them.

▲ The octopus is a predator and can hold onto its prey using the powerful suckers on its tentacles.

Browsers and grazers

The browsers and grazers, such as snails and limpets, use their radulae to scrape food into their mouths. The radula is a membrane that covers a tonguelike structure called the odontophore that is fixed to the floor of the mouth. The radula has many rows of tiny teeth that curve backward into the mouth. The mollusk pushes the odontophore out of its mouth and uses the radula like rough sandpaper to tear off pieces of food. The radula is then withdrawn into the mouth. Here, saliva containing mucus sticks the food particles together. Other substances in the saliva begin to digest, or break down, the food.

Filter feeders

Filter feeding is a characteristic of such bivalves as mussels. Bivalves do not have a distinct head or a radula. They do have well-developed gills, called ctenidia, in the mantle cavity inside the shell. These gills are covered in tiny hairs called cilia. The gills act as strainers. The cilia beat rhythmically, creating a current of water that brings in tiny food particles. Mucus on the gills traps the particles and is moved to the mouth by the cilia. The food is then passed into the digestive system.

Amazing facts

- The radula of a browsing mollusk is continually worn away through use. Special cells produce rows of teeth at the back of the radula. As the new teeth form, the whole structure moves toward the front of the mouth.
- The venom of a cone shell can be fatal to human beings. It is similar to curare, a poison that oozes from certain South American trees and is used to make poison arrows.

Predators

Cephalopods, such as the octopus, are predators. The head is surrounded by tentacles or arms that have suckers on them for catching and holding prey. The mouth has a pair of strong jaws that form a beaklike structure. Inside the mouth, there are two pairs of salivary glands and a radula. One pair of these glands makes venom that is injected into the prey as it is bitten by the jaws.

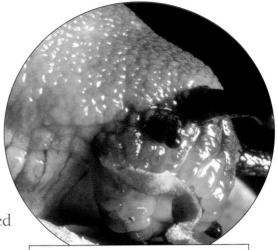

Some gastropods are predators. Cone shells feed on worms, other mollusks, or small fish. They follow the scent of their prey and then use long, sharp teeth to bite and inject it with venom. The paralyzed victim is then swallowed whole. Once a tooth has been used, it usually breaks off and another is brought forward from the radula.

▲ Slugs are grazers that use their radulae to tear off pieces of plant material.

Some gastropods, such as dog whelks, use their radulae to bore holes into the shells of other mollusks. A worm shell produces mucus from its foot. The mucus traps small animals on which the worm shell feeds.

▼ Bivalves, such as this file shell, are filter feeders. They draw water containing food particles over their gills. The particles are trapped by sticky mucus and then swallowed.

Mollusk Classes

Most members of the mollusk phylum have an external shell. In many groups, the shell provides shape and protection for the soft body. Some shells are adapted for burrowing, while others camouflage their owners so that they can avoid predators.

Single shells

Gastropods are the largest group of mollusks that have a single external shell. Examples include the abalone, the cone shell, and the garden snail. In this class, the shell is usually coiled into a spiral, into which the animal can withdraw its body. Many aquatic gastropods have an operculum, a plate that closes and seals the opening of the shell. This protects the animal inside. Slugs have either a very small shell or no shell at all. Gastropods are found all over the world in marine, freshwater, and land habitats. They range in size from a fraction of an inch to more than 9 inches (25 cm) long.

Amazing facts

- Some of the largest gastropods are sea slugs. They can weigh up to about 45 pounds (20 kilograms), which is about three times the weight of an average domestic cat.

- The largest bivalves are giant clams found in the coral reefs of the Indian and Pacific Oceans. They can weigh more than 440 pounds (200 kilograms).

- The gastropod with the largest shell is the Australian trumpet, a snail found in northern Australia. Its shell can be up to 24 inches (60 centimeters) across.

◀ Volute shells have distinctive markings. These gastropods are slow-moving carnivores that spend much of their time buried in mud. They smother prey with their large feet.

▼ The single shell of the garden snail prevents it from drying out and protects it from predators.

Scaphopods, or tusk shells, also have single shells, but they differ from gastropods in several ways. The shells of scaphopods are long, tubular structures that are open at both ends. The shells look like curved tusks with one end wider than the other. Scaphopods do not have eyes, tentacles, or gills. They live in oceans and range in size from 0.08 to 6 inches (0.2 to 15 centimeters) long.

Monoplacophorans are adapted for living at great depths in the oceans, where there is less competition for food and living space from other species. They have cone-shaped shells and no eyes or tentacles. There are very few species, and they range in size from 0.08 to 1.4 inches (0.2 to 3.5 centimeters) in length.

Two shells: the bivalves

Bivalves, such as the edible mussel, have a shell in two parts, or valves. The two valves are joined together by a tough, flexible ligament. The body usually consists of a foot, which is flattened like a wedge, and a large mantle cavity containing prominent gills. Bivalves have no heads and no radulae. Many adult bivalves live attached to rocks and do not move around. They are filter feeders, which means they get food by drawing water through their bodies.

▼ The seashore is home to large numbers of mollusks. On this shore, limpets with single shells live alongside groups of edible mussels.

11

Chitons

Chitons belong to the order Polyplacophora and have external shells made up of eight plates that often overlap. There is a well-developed foot, a head, and gills that allow the chiton to take in oxygen. There are no eyes or tentacles, but some species have sensors in their shells that detect changes in light. A chiton uses its foot to move from one place to another and for clinging onto rocks. If it is detached from the rock, it can roll up into a ball. All chitons are marine. Many live on rocky shores and others live in deep water. They are grazers that use their radula to scrape algae from rock surfaces.

▲ The overlapping plates of the chiton's shell can clearly be seen in this photograph.

No external shells

The class Aplacophora contains wormlike mollusks without shells. They do not look much like other mollusks because they do not have a foot and the head is poorly developed. However, they do have a radula. The body is surrounded by a tough covering containing tiny pieces of chalky material. These mollusks are found burrowing through sediment and feeding on small animals or their remains.

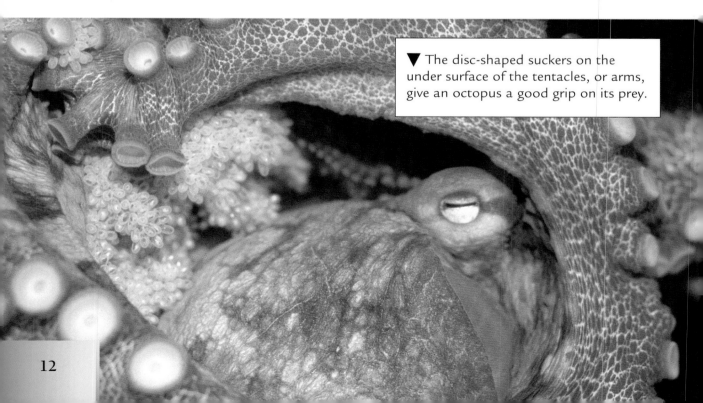

▼ The disc-shaped suckers on the under surface of the tentacles, or arms, give an octopus a good grip on its prey.

Cephalopods

The characteristic feature of cephalopods is the presence of tentacles, or arms, around the mouth. The only cephalopods to have true external shells are nautiluses. Cuttlefish, squid, and octopuses have either an internal shell or no shell. Cephalopods vary greatly in shape. Most are streamlined and their foot forms a funnel that can remove water rapidly from the mantle cavity. The water is pushed out like a jet, so some of these mollusks can move very quickly. Many cephalopods can change color and some can produce an inklike substance when they are threatened by a predator. The ink makes the water cloudy and hides the cephalopod from the predator, allowing it to escape.

A primitive mollusk

Using knowledge of the features of living mollusks, scientists have tried to determine what the ancestor of modern mollusks would have looked like. It is quite likely that this ancient relative lived in shallow seas, crawled over rocks, and fed on algae. These creatures were probably small, oval in shape, and protected by a shell that could be clamped down on the rocks. These primitive mollusks are thought to have been able to crawl using a muscular foot. They were able to scrape their food from the rocks using their radulae. The modern limpet would be the closest living mollusk to this primitive ancestor.

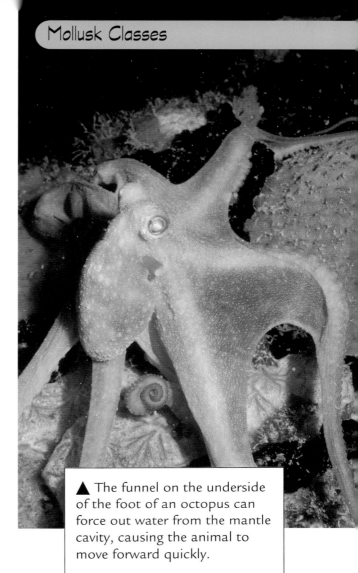

▲ The funnel on the underside of the foot of an octopus can force out water from the mantle cavity, causing the animal to move forward quickly.

Amazing facts

- The zebra mussel is an invasive species found in large numbers (up to 100,000 per square yard) in parts of the Columbia River.
- The body of the blind deep-sea octopus is like that of a jellyfish. It is so transparent that a page of a newspaper can be read through it.

Gastropods

About 80 percent of all mollusks are gastropods. They range in size from tiny snails to large sea slugs that can weigh up to 30 pounds (13 kilograms). Gastropods are found in marine, freshwater, and land habitats all over the world. A typical gastropod has a single shell, a muscular foot, a well-developed head with eyes and tentacles, and a radula. The shell is usually coiled into a spiral, although slugs have small shells or no shells at all.

Gastropods are divided into three subclasses: prosobranchs, opisthobranchs, and pulmonates. Prosobranchs are the oldest group. The other two groups are thought to have evolved from this one.

Aquatic gastropods

Most gastropods are prosobranchs that have typical gastropod features. Prosobranchs, such as limpets and cone shells, are mostly found in marine habitats. However, there are some land-dwelling and freshwater species. Prosobranchs have only one pair of tentacles on their heads and their eyes are at the base of these tentacles. All opisthobranchs are marine animals. The more primitive members of the group have coiled shells, but in many species the shell is small or there is no shell. Some species are brightly colored and have external **gills**.

Classification key

PHYLUM	Mollusca
CLASS	**Gastropoda**
SUBCLASSES	3 – Prosobranchia (abalones, limpets, and cone shells), Opisthobranchia (sea hares, sea slugs, and bubble shells), and Pulmonata (land snails and slugs)
ORDERS	15
SPECIES	about 75,000

▼ The leopard slug is a gastropod without a shell. It gets its name from its distinctive markings.

▲ Ramshorn snails are pulmonates that live in freshwater and breathe air. They can survive in stagnant water that has a low oxygen content as well as in fast-flowing streams.

Pulmonates

Pulmonates can be separated from the other two major groups of gastropods because they do not have an operculum or gills. The mantle cavity has adapted to form a lung. Pulmonates have two pairs of tentacles. The eyes are located at the ends of the longer pair of tentacles. The shorter pair of tentacles can detect smells and help the mollusk to find its food. Many land pulmonates have external shells that may be patterned or brightly colored. Some land slugs have internal shells, but they are very small and contained within the mantle.

Amazing facts

- *Gastropod* means "stomach foot" and refers to the position of the stomach immediately above the muscular foot.
- Garden snails move at speeds of around 0.04 miles (0.06 kilometers) per hour.
- The ancient Romans fattened snails for food by feeding them bran soaked in wine.

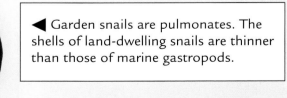

◄ Garden snails are pulmonates. The shells of land-dwelling snails are thinner than those of marine gastropods.

Marine Gastropods

The distribution of marine gastropods depends on their food supply. The browsers and grazers, such as limpets and top shells, feed on seaweed or other small algae. They are therefore found on rocky shores, in rock pools, or in shallow coastal waters where there is enough light for such plants to grow. Light cannot reach the deeper waters, so there are no plants available. Predatory gastropods, such as venomous cone shells and some sea slugs, are found mostly in shallow coastal waters and coral reefs where there is plenty of food. Some species, such as dog whelks, are found in the intertidal zone, the area of the shore that is covered and exposed by the tides. There they prey on other gastropods and arthropods.

Classification key	
SUBCLASS	**Prosobranchia**
ORDERS	4
FAMILIES	51
SPECIES	7,000

Rocky shores

Rocky shores are very specialized habitats that have clear zones of vegetation associated with different prosobranch gastropods. In the United States, for example, the black periwinkle and the rough periwinkle graze on lichens and tiny algae in the splash zone, the area of the shore furthest from the sea. They have thick, tough shells that protect them from waves and from drying out. They can survive extremes of temperature and attach themselves firmly to the rocks when the sea is at its roughest. If they are dislodged from their rocks by waves and washed down the shore towards the sea, they move back up to their previous positions.

▼ Blue-rayed limpets are small marine gastropods that graze on seaweed on the seashore.

In the middle of the intertidal zone, the flat periwinkle is found feeding on bladder wrack, a type of seaweed. This periwinkle cannot survive in the conditions higher up the shore, but it is well adapted to living on the seaweed of the middle shore. It is covered by the tide for longer and the temperature is less variable.

Limpets are herbivores that have adapted to cope with conditions on the middle and lower regions of rocky shores. These areas of the shore are covered by the tide for longer periods. The limpets rotate their shells on the rock surface and grind out a dent into which they fit. Each limpet has its own dent, where it returns after grazing. At low tide, the muscular foot clamps down firmly to the surface of the rocks so that water is not lost and the limpet is protected from predators and waves.

▼ Dog whelks eat other mollusks such as mussels, limpets, and barnacles.

▲ Flat periwinkles are found grazing on bladder wrack. They change color to stay camouflaged when the colors of the seaweed changes during the different seasons.

Amazing facts

- Dog whelks have a radula adapted for making holes in the shells of limpets and other mollusks.
- The black periwinkle can tolerate temperatures of up to 104 °F (40 °C) in the splash zone of a rocky shore.

Sea Slugs

Sea slugs and their relatives are gastropods that have little or no shell. The most primitive groups have coiled shells, but most adult sea slugs have no shells. The major groups of sea slugs include bubble shells, sea hares, sacoglossans, side-gilled slugs, and nudibranchs (naked gills).

▲ This brightly colored dorid nudibranch is oval in shape and has a large number of feathery gills on its back.

The shell of a sea hare is simply a horny structure embedded in the mantle, and it is not visible. The North Atlantic sea hare crawls around on the seabed among the seaweed. It can swim using flaps along the sides of its body and grows up to 12 inches (30 centimeters) long.

Nudibranchs are very colorful marine gastropods that can be divided into two groups: dorids and eolids. Dorids are oval-shaped and have feathery gills on their backs. Eolids are more elongated and have no gills. On their backs are outgrowths of fine tubes called cerata. The cerata contain stinging cells that the eolids obtain from the sea anemones and jellyfish that they eat. When an eolid is attacked, it can sting its attacker using these stinging cells.

Rocky shores

The sea lemon has a mottled, yellowish body and is sometimes found on the lower rocky shores of the United Kingdom in the summer months. It feeds on the breadcrumb sponges that grow under boulders. The gray sea slug is commonly found under stones on the shore, and it feeds on sea anemones.

◀ This sea lemon is feeding on a breadcrumb sponge.

Classification key

PHYLUM	Mollusca
CLASS	Gastropoda
SUBCLASS	**Opisthobranchia**
ORDERS	9
FAMILIES	107
GENERA	168
SPECIES	approximately 2,000

Amazing facts

- The largest nudibranch in the world is the orange peel nudibranch, which can reach 12 inches (30 centimeters) in length. It feeds on orange sea pens and soft coral.
- When disturbed, the sea hare can squirt a violet dye into the water. This hides it from its enemies for a few moments, giving it time to escape.

Coral reefs

Many sea slugs live on coral reefs. Some feed on the corals, but others are herbivores. The lettuce sea slug is a saccoglossan. It feeds on algae that grow on the reef. The teeth on the radula slice open the cells of the algae and suck up the liquid inside. The green substance in the liquid is stored in the slug's digestive system, making it look green. This substance, called chlorophyll, is used by the algae to trap energy from sunlight and make food. It continues to work once it is inside the sea slug.

▲ The lettuce slug is camouflaged to look like a leaf. It has no shell and it breathes through its skin.

Land Gastropods

Land gastropods include garden snails and slugs. Snails all have external shells. Some slugs have small, internal shells and one group, called semislugs, have a tiny external shell perched on the end of the foot. The shells of most land snails are camouflaged so that they can blend in with their surroundings and avoid predators.

Most land gastropods are active at night. Their bodies lose moisture easily, and they need water to make mucus, the slime that helps them to move smoothly. During the day, snails withdraw into their shells and stick themselves to the undersides of pots, stones, or logs to reduce water loss. Slugs squeeze themselves into small spaces under bark and into spaces between stones.

Land gastropods do not have gills. The mantle cavity is adapted to form a lung. Air is drawn into the mantle cavity through an external opening, called the pneumostome, which can also be closed to reduce water loss.

Classification key	
PHYLUM	Mollusca
CLASS	Gastropoda
SUBCLASS	**Pulmonata**
ORDER	4
FAMILIES	36
GENERA	103

Survival strategies

During very dry weather and in cold winters, snails seal the openings of their shells with a layer of mucus that becomes hard and waterproof. Inside the sealed shell, the snail can survive for several months. Snails that live in warmer climates where the ground becomes hot in summer climb up into the vegetation. Then they close off the opening to their shells so that they do not lose too much water. This behavior, called estivation, allows the snails to survive until conditions become more favorable. Slugs usually burrow underground when conditions are dry.

◀ The sticky mucus produced by this kerry slug protects its foot as it crawls over the ground.

◀ The shell of the banded snail is camouflaged so that it blends in with the vegetation in which it lives.

Moving around on land

Slugs and snails, like all gastropods, move by means of wavelike contractions of the muscles in the foot. As the muscles tighten, they pull the flat part of the foot into a series of tiny ridges, pushing the animal forward. Mucus is produced from special glands on the bottom of the foot. The mucus helps the snail or slug slide along the ground and protects the soft tissues of the foot from being damaged by sharp stones. The mucus is very sticky and helps the gastropods to grip surfaces. It helps them climb up walls and over objects.

Amazing facts

- Slugs were once used as a cure for warts. The wart was rubbed with the slug and then the slug was impaled on a thorn. The wart was supposed to disappear as the slug died and withered.
- The largest land snail is the giant African land snail, whose extended body can reach a length of 8 inches (20 centimeters).

▶ The moss on this rock is providing a good supply of food for this snail.

Bivalves

Bivalves are found in marine and freshwater habitats all over the world. They range in size from tiny clams about 0.02 inches (0.5 millimeters) long to the giant clam, which can grow to lengths of more than 3 feet (1 meter). Their main characteristic is a shell made up of two halves, or valves, joined by a hinge.

◀ The cockle is more spherical than many bivalves, with the two valves very similar in shape. Ridges form a fanlike pattern on each half of the shell.

Two halves

The two valves of the bivalve shell are held together by a flexible, tough ligament. The valves can be closed by powerful muscles attached to the inside of the shell. When the bivalve is at rest, the muscles are relaxed and the valves are open. Usually there are two sets of these muscles, but scallops have only a single, central set.

Bivalve features

Bivalves do not have heads or radulae. There are often simple sense organs that are sensitive to touch and to differences in light. These are found on small tentacles along the edges of the mantle. Bivalves are filter feeders. Food particles are trapped in mucus on the ctenidia, or gills. The food is then transferred to a pair of appendages, called labial palps, which push it into the mouth. Most bivalves feed on tiny algae and animals, as well as on the decaying remains of plants and animals.

Classification key

PHYLUM	Mollusca
CLASS	**Bivalvia**
ORDERS	10
FAMILIES	114
SPECIES	about 15,000

◀ The shells of edible oysters are often covered with other marine animals and plants.

Bivalves have a muscular foot, but it is wedge-shaped and not used to glide along as it is in gastropods. It is used either for attachment or for burrowing. In some bivalves, such as mussels, the foot produces byssal threads. These are made of tough protein and anchor the mussel to the rocks. Other bivalves, such as cockles, use their feet for burrowing into soft sand.

Most bivalves use their ctenidia to take in oxygen, which they need for their essential body functions and for trapping food. A current of water is drawn across the surface of the ctenidia so that oxygen can be absorbed. The water is drawn into the animal by a muscular tube called the inhalant siphon. The water passes over the ctenidia and then leaves through another tube called the exhalant siphon.

Amazing facts

- Scallops can swim away from danger, opening and closing their shells to push themselves along. However, most bivalves shut themselves up inside their shells for protection.
- The spiny cockle can leap distances of up to 4 inches (10 centimeters) if its shell is touched by a predator such as a sea star.

▼ Bivalves such as mussels open under water to show the edges of the mantle.

Rock busters

Piddocks live in burrows. They have bean-shaped shells with rough teeth on the front edges of the valves. As their bodies twist and turn, they open and close their shells in order to drill burrows in solid rock. The outer layers of the shell are worn away by the drilling, so the piddock moves its mantle over the worn shell and makes a new layer. Date mussels can also insert themselves into solid rock, but they do not use the same method as piddocks. Instead of drilling their way in, they produce chemicals that dissolve the rock. They can be found in the hard coral reefs of the Red Sea.

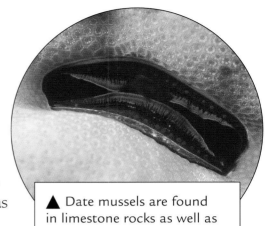

▲ Date mussels are found in limestone rocks as well as in coral reefs.

A diet of sawdust

Shipworms can make holes in wooden structures such as the hulls of boats and the underwater foundations of jetties. These bivalves feed on the sawdust from the wood they drill out. Their bodies are elongated and wormlike, with the shell reduced to two small valves at the front end of the animal. These valves act like a drill to bore into the wood. The mantle covers the body behind the shell and forms a hard, chalky tube in which the shipworm lives. Shipworms are more common in warm waters, where their bodies may grow to over 7 feet (2 meters) long.

▼ The piddock can drill its way into rock using the sharp edges of the two parts of its shell.

Sand burrowers

The common razor shell clam, *Ensis ensis*, is found on sandy shores. It grows to more than 5 feet (13 centimeters) long and is able to burrow into the sand quickly with its flexible, muscular foot. When burrowing, the foot is elongated and pushed down into the sand as far as it will go. The tip of the foot swells and anchors the razor shell. The foot muscles then tighten and pull the shell down into the sand. This action is repeated until the animal is completely buried.

The soft-shelled clam or steamer clam is found burrowing in areas of sand and mud in the intertidal zone of the shore. It has thin, fragile valves that are up to 6 inches (15 centimeters) long, and it is usually found about 4 to 12 inches (10 to 30 centimeters) below the surface. Soft-shelled clams may live for 12 years.

▶ The elongated foot of the razor shell enables it to burrow quickly into soft sand.

Amazing facts

- Razor shells, or razor clams, are dug out of the sand as food for people. They are located by the dent left on the surface of the sand. This dent shows where the shell has been pulled down.
- Shipworms can make holes more than 0.5 inches (2 centimeters) wide in the bottoms of wooden boats.

The Giant Clam

The giant clam is the largest bivalve mollusk. It grows up to 3 feet (1 meter) in diameter. It is found in the Pacific and Indian Oceans, and is most common in the warm waters of shallow lagoons and in coral reefs. It can live at depths of up to 65 feet (20 meters).

Giant clams stay fixed in one place. Their shells are thick and heavy and they lie with their hinge downward on the seabed. The mantle may be golden brown, yellow, or green, with purple, blue, or green spots around the edges. There are also pale or clear spots, called windows, on the mantle. If the clams are disturbed, the brightly colored mantle tissue is withdrawn inside the shell, and the valves close together.

Classification key

PHYLUM	Mollusca
CLASS	Bivalvia
ORDER	Veneroida
FAMILY	Tridacnidae
GENUS	*Tridacna*
SPECIES	***Tridacna gigas***

Feeding

The giant clam obtains most of its food from the single-celled algae that live in the outer tissue of its mantle. These algae give the mantle of the giant clam its color. The algae use energy from sunlight to make food for the clam, and the clam provides protection and shelter for the algae. Both the clam and the algae benefit from the relationship. The clam will die if there are no algae, or if it is kept in the dark. If the algae have no light they cannot make the food. The windows in the mantle of the clam are thought to let in more light for the algae. The giant clam is also a filter feeder, using its ctenidia to sift food from the water.

▶ The clam uses its powerful muscles to open and close the two halves of the shell. These muscles are a source of food for people living on the islands of the South Pacific.

Reproduction

Reproduction in giant clams occurs when male and female sex cells are released into the sea. Fertilization takes place in the open water. The fertilized eggs develop into veliger larvae. The larvae swim and feed in the open water until they are big enough to settle on sand or part of the reef. They begin their adult lives fixed in one place.

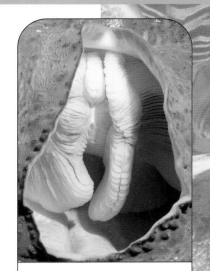

▲ The giant clam is a filter feeder. A current of water is drawn into the clam's body and tiny organisms are sifted from the water by its gills.

◄ The exposed mantle of the giant clam contains large numbers of tiny algae that make food for the clam.

Amazing facts

- A giant clam found on the Great Barrier Reef off the coast of Australia measured 3 feet (1 meter) across and was estimated to weigh about 550 pounds (250 kilograms).
- Many people believe that a giant clam can snap shut very quickly, trapping divers by their legs and causing them to drown. In fact, clams close their valves quite slowly. There are no real cases of people being trapped by them.

Cephalopods

Cephalopod means "head-foot" and describes the position of the head being surrounded by the foot. Cephalopods have adapted to become fast-moving predators with highly developed sense organs. Most species, with the exception of the nautilus, appear very different from primitive mollusks. Scientists believe that the ancestors of the octopus, squid, and cuttlefish evolved from nautiluslike forms about 438 million years ago, before there were fish in the sea and trees on land.

Cephalopods are all found in marine habitats, from warm, tropical waters to polar regions. Squid live mainly in the open sea, but most cuttlefish and octopuses prefer the seabed close to the shore. There are open-ocean octopuses, though, such as the giant Pacific octopus, which is found at depths of 2,500 feet (750 meters). Nautiluses are mostly found in deep, tropical waters.

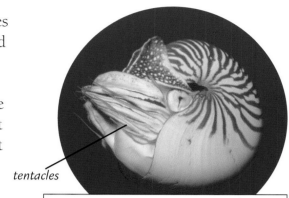

tentacles

▲ The nautilus differs from other cephalopods. It has many more tentacles surrounding the mouth. These tentacles do not have suckers.

Classification key

PHYLUM	Mollusca
CLASS	**Cephalopoda**
SUBCLASS	2–Coleoidea (octopuses, squid, and cuttlefish) and nautiloidea (nautiluses)
ORDERS	5
SPECIES	about 660

▼ The internal shell of the cuttlefish is a buoyancy organ that helps the animal to keep its position in the water.

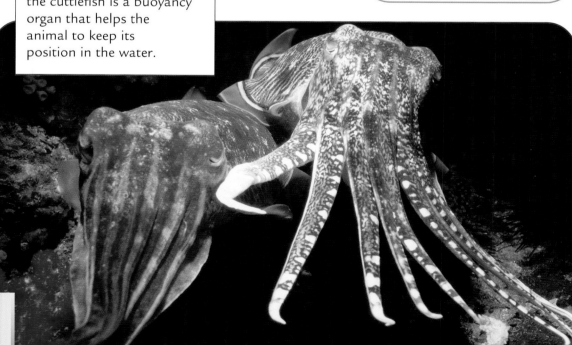

◄ During the day, octopuses hide among the rocks. They can use the suckers on their arms to grip the rock and pull themselves along.

Cephalopod features

Cephalopods are carnivores that feed on fish, crustaceans, and other mollusks that they catch with their tentacles. The cephalopods range in size from male argonauts with a length of 0.4 inches (10 millimeters) to the giant squid that can grow to about 65 feet (20 meters) long.

The characteristic features of the cephalopods include the presence of tentacles with suckers, well-developed eyes, a radula, and a pair of jaws that form a beaklike mouth. The head is large and surrounded by tentacles that are used to search for and capture prey. The tentacles are formed from the front part of the foot. Mating follows a complicated courtship. The female lays fertilized eggs with large yolks. There are no free-swimming larval stages, and the young hatch as miniature adults.

Amazing facts

- The cuttlebone from cuttlefish is sold in pet shops as a source of calcium for birds.

- Many cephalopods have special cells called chromatophores in their skin. These cells allow the cephalopod to change color and blend into its background to escape from predators.

- Most cephalopods have well-developed eyes with a single lens. Their eyes can form clear, sharp images. The eye of a nautilus does not have a lens. It works like a pinhole camera and can form only a dim image.

The Octopus

Octopuses are found in all the oceans of the world, but they are most common in tropical and subtropical seas. Most octopuses live on the seabed, where they hunt crustaceans and other mollusks. The smallest octopus, *Octopus micropyrsus*, has a body length of less than one inch (2.5 centimeters), while the body length of some octopuses found in the North Pacific may exceed 3 feet (1 meter).

Octopus features

Octopuses have eight tentacles, or arms, set around a beaklike mouth. They differ from other cephalopods, such as squid and cuttlefish, because they do not have a pair of long arms. Octopuses crawl around on the seabed using the suckers on their arms to grip rocks. When they need to move quickly, they swim backward by squirting water out of their funnels.

Octopuses have well-developed brains, excellent eyesight, and a great sense of touch, but there is no evidence to suggest that they can react to sound. Their eyes are similar in structure to the eyes of vertebrates, with a large lens forming clear images on a part of the eye called the retina. In the vertebrate eye, the image is brought into focus by changing the shape of the lens. In the eye of the octopus, the image is brought into focus by the lens moving backward and forward in the eyeball.

Classification key

PHYLUM	Mollusca
CLASS	Cephalopoda
SUBCLASS	Coleoidea
ORDER	Dibranchiata
SUBORDER	Octopoda
FAMILY	Octopodidae
GENUS	***Octopus* and others, including *Eledone* and *Cirrothauma***
SPECIES	150

▼ The body of an octopus is short and rounded, and there is no internal shell. The arms have two rows of suckers.

Masters of disguise

Octopuses can change color quickly due to special cells called chromatophores in their skin. An octopus has two kinds of chromatophores: one kind changes from black to red-brown and the other kind changes from red to orange-yellow. Combinations of these colors mean that an octopus can blend in with its background and escape predators. If disturbed, the octopus can also release a dark, inky fluid into the water. This hides it from the predator and gives it time to escape.

Amazing facts

- The largest giant Pacific octopus ever caught weighed around 600 pounds (270 kilograms) and had an arm span of about 30 feet (10 meters).
- The female common octopus lays between 200,000 and 400,000 tiny eggs at a time. Only one or two survive to become adults.
- When kept in aquariums, octopuses have shown the ability to use trial and error to solve problems, such as finding food in a maze. Once a problem has been solved, they can remember it and are able to solve similar problems.

▼ The blue-ringed octopus has a venomous bite. This small octopus reaches about 4 inches (10 centimeters) in length and is found off the coast of Australia. It feeds on crabs and prawns.

▲ The paper nautilus is an octopus that looks like a nautilus. Breeding females have thin shells that help them take care of the fertilized eggs.

Cuttlefish and Squid

Like all cephalopods, cuttlefish and squid are carnivorous. They all have beaklike mouths surrounded by eight short tentacles, or arms, and two longer ones used for catching prey. They have internal shell,s a radulae, and streamlined bodies with fins along the sides. They use the fins for swimming, but can also move more rapidly by forcing water through the funnel.

Cuttlefish

Cuttlefish live on the seabed fairly close to the shore. They prefer sandy areas where they can bury themselves during the day and come out at night to hunt. The shell of the cuttlefish, called the cuttlebone, is contained within the mantle. Extra layers are added to the cuttlebone throughout the life of the cuttlefish. The cuttlebone has hollows in it that are filled with gas and fluids, and it works as a buoyancy organ. The proportions of gas and fluid can be controlled by the cuttlefish, allowing it to hover at a certain depth while looking for prey. The cuttlebone also provides a place for muscle attachment and gives support to the body.

Cuttlefish have shorter, broader bodies than squid do. The body is slightly flattened from top to bottom. Extending down the side of the body are paired fins cuttlefish use when swimming slowly. The inner surfaces of the short tentacles and the ends of the elongated ones are covered in short, round suckers.

Classification key

PHYLUM	Mollusca
CLASS	Cephalopoda
SUBCLASS	Coleoidea
ORDER	**Sepioida (cuttlefish)**
FAMILIES	5
SPECIES	about 150
ORDER	**Teuthoida (squid)**
FAMILIES	12
SPECIES	about 500

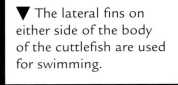
▼ The lateral fins on either side of the body of the cuttlefish are used for swimming.

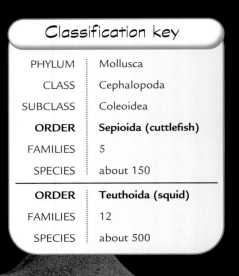

Squid

Squid are more powerful swimmers than cuttlefish. They live in the open seas, often at great depths. They have streamlined, torpedo-shaped bodies with diamond-shaped fins at the rear end. The internal shell, a horny structure called a pen, is found under the mantle on the upper surface of the animal.

Many squid species have bodies less than 10 inches (25 centimeters) long. However, the giant squid, *Architeuthis harveyi*, may reach lengths of 60 feet (18 meters)and weigh up to 2,000 pounds (900 kilograms). Giant squid have been seen in the Pacific and North Atlantic oceans. They are thought to live at the bottom of the ocean, feeding on fish, crustaceans, and other, smaller squid. Many squid species hunt alone but some, such as the Pacific squid, may hunt in schools.

▼ Cuttlefish have eight short tentacles, or arms, and two that are elongated. The elongated tentacles have broader ends and can be moved rapidly. Prey is caught and held by the suckers on the ends of these longer tentacles and then drawn toward the mouth.

Amazing facts

- Like the octopus, squid and cuttlefish can change color to blend in with their background and will release an inky, black fluid if disturbed.
- Some species of squid that live near the surface have been observed to shoot out of the water and glide for distances of up to 145 feet (45 meters).
- The eyes of the giant squid are the largest in the animal kingdom, measuring up to 10 inches (25 centimeters) in diameter.

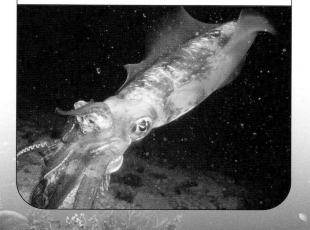

▼ Squid have more torpedo-shaped bodies than cuttlefish.

33

The Nautilus

The Nautiloidea are an ancient group of cephalopods, and *Nautilus* is the only surviving genus. It is the only genus of cephalopods with an external shell. Today, there are five species found in the warm, tropical waters of the Indian and Pacific Oceans. They rest on the ocean floor during the day and swim around at night to catch their prey. Nautiluses hunt crustaceans, such as shrimp, and small fish. Like other cephalopods, nautiluses swim by using jet propulsion.

▶ The nautilus is found in the Pacific and Indian Oceans.

Classification key

PHYLUM	Mollusca
CLASS	Cephalopoda
SUBCLASS	Nautiloidea
ORDER	Nautilida
FAMILY	1–Nautilidae
GENUS	*Nautilus*
SPECIES	5

Many tentacles

The nautilus is similar to other cephalopods because it has a head with tentacles around the mouth, beaklike jaws, and a radula. It differs from other cephalopods because it has many more tentacles —up to 90 in two rows. These tentacles are small, sticky, and able to contract, but they do not have suckers. The eyes of the nautilus are large, but they are simple and do not have lenses. Around the eyes are tentacles called ocular tentacles, which are are sensitive to touch and protect the animal's eyes.

▶ This cutaway view of the nautilus shell shows the chambers that have been added as it has grown.

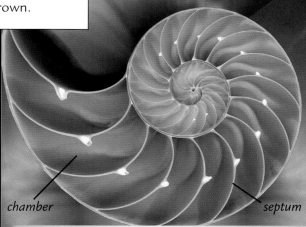

chamber   septum

The nautilus shell

The shell of the nautilus is smooth and coiled. It can grow to a diameter of 11 inches (28 centimeters). The shell is lined with nacre, or mother-of-pearl, and consists of a number of gas-filled chambers. The animal occupies the outermost, largest chamber of its shell. A speckled, fleshy hood above the head covers part of the shell. When the head is withdrawn into the shell, the hood covers the opening and protects the animal from predators.

As the nautilus grows, more chambers are formed by the mantle and added to the shell. The previous chamber is sealed off by a wall, called a septum. When a chamber is first sealed off, it is completely filled with fluid. This fluid is gradually replaced by a mixture of gases. The nautilus can vary the amounts of **gases and fluids in the chambers of its shell** to change its buoyancy.

Amazing facts

- The shell of the nautilus is incredibly strong and can withstand pressure more than five times greater than normal atmospheric pressure.
- About 510 million years ago, the ancestors of the nautilus were the largest predators in the seas.

▶ The nautilus feeds on shrimp and fish that it catches with its tentacles.

Minor Classes of Mollusks

The most familiar mollusks, such as slugs and snails, mussels, and octopuses, belong to the three major classes: Gastropoda, Bivalvia, and Cephalopoda. In these classes there are many different species and some of the species have very large populations. The minor classes have both fewer species and smaller populations. All the species are marine. The Monoplacophora were believed to be extinct until the middle of the 20th century and, together with the Aplacophora and Scaphopoda, contain only a few species. The minor classes show how varied the phylum is and also show how the groups have evolved in different ways. This is why it is so difficult to create a picture of a typical mollusk.

Aplacophorans

These marine mollusks are wormlike, with poorly developed heads, no eyes, and no shells. They are covered in a tough sheath that has tiny, chalky crystals in it. Aplacophorans have no foot or mantle, but they do have a radula. They live on the seabed or in coral reefs. Some species are predators and others feed on particles of plants and dead animals. Their size ranges from 0.04 to 12 inches (1 millimeter to 30 centimeters). Some scientists divide this class into two groups: the solenogasters and the caudofoveatans. Solenogasters are wormlike mollusks that live in the deep sea and are often found around corals. Caudofoveatans are burrowers that feed on small animals and on decaying plants and animals.

Classification key

PHYLUM	Mollusca
CLASS	Aplacophora (or Solenogasters and Caudofoveata)
ORDERS	3
FAMILIES	24
SPECIES	about 250

▼ With their external shell of eight overlapping plates, chitons are thought to resemble ancestral mollusks.

Amazing facts

- *Cryptochiton stelleri* is found in the waters from northern California to Alaska. It is the world's largest species of chiton and can reach a length of about 12 inches (30 centimeters).
- Tusk shells of the genus *Dentalium* were used as money by the Native Americans of the Pacific coast until the 19th century.

Monoplacophorans

Monoplacophorans were thought to have become extinct more than 300 million years ago. In May of 1952, a Danish research ship hauled up a number of living specimens off the coast of Mexico. Since then, a number of different species have been found. Monoplacophorans are small, primitive mollusks ranging in length from 0.11 to 1.2 inches (3 to 30 millimeters). They have caplike shells and a muscular foot. The shell is very thin with a mother-of-pearl inner surface and a yellowish-white outer surface. Inside, these mollusks show signs of division into segments. This has led some scientists to believe that mollusks might have evolved from marine annelids, or segmented worms.

Classification key	
PHYLUM	Mollusca
CLASS	**Monoplacophora**
ORDERS	1
FAMILIES	1
SPECIES	11

Polyplacophorans (chitons)

Chitons are marine mollusks that live in the intertidal zone of rocky shores. They feed on algae that they scrape off the rocks with their radulae. They have a flattened, oval shape and a shell made up of eight overlapping plates, or valves, surrounded by a supporting outer ring formed by the mantle.

Classification key	
PHYLUM	Mollusca
CLASS	**Polyplacophora (chitons)**
ORDERS	3
FAMILIES	13
SPECIES	about 600

Scaphopods (tusk shells)

This class of marine mollusks lives on the seabed in sand or mud. They have elongated, tubular shells that are open at both ends. The head is not well developed and they have no eyes or tentacles. The adults search for food with their heads buried in the sand or mud. Food is caught using fine, needle-like filaments covered in cilia. These filaments can tighten in order to move food into the mouth, where there is a large radula.

Classification key	
PHYLUM	Mollusca
CLASS	**Scaphopoda (tusk shells)**
ORDERS	2
FAMILIES	8
SPECIES	550

▶ Tusk shells have elongated bodies with reduced heads. They spend their lives feeding on plant and animal remains on the seabed.

Mollusks Under Threat

Many mollusks are under threat of becoming extinct. It is thought that 34 bivalve species and 264 gastropod species have become extinct since the middle of the 20th century. More than 50 bivalve species and 170 gastropod species have been listed as critically endangered by the World Conservation Union (IUCN).

Coral reefs are home to many marine mollusks. In places where supplies of wood or stone for building are limited, coral reefs are sometimes broken up to provide building materials. Reefs are also damaged by snorkelers and divers and polluted by sewage and oil spills.

Pollution of the oceans by sewage and industrial wastes is a serious problem. In many parts of the world, waste is dumped into the sea and leakages occur from underwater pipelines. Oil spills from tankers and underwater pipelines destroy organisms, and poisonous chemicals getting into the water can build up in food chains.

Similar problems affect mollusks in freshwater habitats. Pesticides, herbicides, and fertilizers can run off fields into streams and ponds. Mollusks can be killed directly by chemical pollution or affected by changes in the food chain. Changes such as the draining of marshes to create more farmland can mean that important habitats for mollusks are destroyed.

▼ Large shells are removed from coral reefs to satisfy the demand from collectors.

Hunting and collecting

Seashells are collected by many people to be made into ornaments and jewelry. They have even been used instead of money. Most shells sold in shops to collectors have been taken from living animals. If too many mollusks are removed from one place, such as a coral reef, there is a danger of a species becoming extinct. This is a particular threat to mollusks such as nautiluses, helmet shells, and murexes because people like to collect the bigger, more unusual shells.

Overharvesting of mollusks for food is a threat to certain species. Mussels, clams, scallops, and oysters are among the most popular bivalves eaten by human beings.

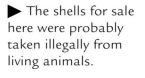

▶ The shells for sale here were probably taken illegally from living animals.

Introduced species

When people introduce one animal species to an area in order to control the numbers of another species, they can disrupt populations within ecosystems. For example, zebra mussels, which were introduced to North America from Eastern Europe, reproduce much faster than native mussels do, and they also compete with them for food and living space. They can kill the native mussels by holding their shells closed to stop them from taking in oxygen and food.

Amazing facts

○ Oysters and other bivalves formed part of the diet of prehistoric humans. Large mounds of shells have been found in many coastal areas near prehistoric settlements around the world.

○ Cone shells are prized for their beautiful patterns, but they have poisonous teeth that can harm unwary collectors who try to collect live specimens.

◀ Zebra mussels do not appear to have any natural enemies or to be sensitive to poor water conditions. Therefore, they can thrive in areas where other mussel species may struggle.

Protecting Mollusks

There are many ways to prevent mollusks from becoming extinct. In order to protect them, it is important to protect their natural habitats and to study the stages of their life cycles and the foods they eat. Some mollusks are considered pests, and it is important to make sure that the steps taken to control them do not disrupt food chains or interfere with habitats.

Marine sanctuaries and guided trips to coastal areas such as coral reefs help to inform people of the importance of preserving aquatic habitats. The conservation of coral reefs, limiting the collection of mollusks for their shells, and controlling the activities of divers can reduce the threats to endangered species.

▼ Guided trips to coral reefs help to protect the environments of endangered species.

Breeding programs

One way of conserving endangered species is to breed them in captivity and eventually release them back into their natural habitats. The white abalone, a species native to California, is endangered. Attempts to breed these snails in captivity have been somewhat successful. By 2004, the National Marine Fisheries Service White Abalone Recovery Team had developed a recovery plan that included breeding white abalone in captivity and then releasing them back into the wild. At that time, the team was raising about 100,000 small white abalone at the Channel Islands Marine Research Institute.

▲ In some parts of the world, amber snails are threatened by introduced snail species that compete for food and space.

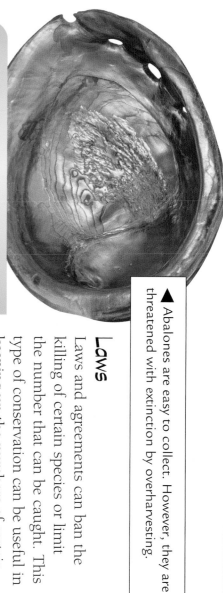

▲ Abalones are easy to collect. However, they are threatened with extinction by overharvesting.

Amazing facts

- Abalones take a long time to reach maturity. They are not able to reproduce until they are six years old. Many are collected before they reach this age, and this has contributed to the decline in their numbers.

- Soft-shell clams are caught for food. In the United States, the legal harvest size is about 2 inches (5 centimeters) in diameter. Any smaller clams that are caught must be returned to the sea.

Laws

Laws and agreements can ban the killing of certain species or limit the number that can be caught. This type of conservation can be useful in keeping up the numbers of certain species of mollusks. In California, strict laws control the abalone industry in order to prevent this mollusk's extinction. It is illegal to remove abalones under a minimum length. This law gives the abalones time to reach maturity and reproduce before they are collected. A ban on the export of abalone meat from the state of California means that the number of people who can buy it is limited. This, in turn, discourages people from collecting abalones to sell.

Classification

Scientists know of about two million different kinds of animals. With so many species, it is important that they be classified into groups so that they can be described more accurately. The groups show how living organisms are related through evolution and where they belong in the natural world. A scientist identifies an animal by looking at features such as the number of legs or the type of teeth. Animals that share the same characteristics belong to the same species. Scientists place species with similar characteristics in the same genus. The genera are grouped together in families, which in turn are grouped into orders, and orders are grouped into classes. Classes are grouped together in phyla and finally, phyla are grouped into kingdoms. Kingdoms are the largest groups. There are five kingdoms: monerans (bacteria), protists (single-celled organisms), fungi, plants, and animals.

Naming an animal

Each species has a unique Latin name that consists of two words. The first word is the name of the genus to which the organism belongs. The second is the name of its species. For example, the Latin name of the marble cone shell is *Conus marmoreus* and that of the striated cone shell is *Conus striatus*. This tells us that these animals are grouped in the same genus but are different species. Latin names are used to avoid confusion. Abalones, gastropods found off the west coast of North America, are called ormers, awabis, or ear-shells, depending on where you happen to be. Sometimes there are very small differences between individuals that belong to the same species, so there is an extra division called a subspecies. To show that an animal belongs to a subspecies, another name is added to the end of the Latin name. For example, there are two subspecies of the snail *Partula suturalis: Partula suturalis strigosa* and *Partula suturalis vexillum*.

▶ There are many snail species. However, they all have a spiral shell and muscular foot.

This table shows how a common limpet is classified.

Classification	Example: common limpet	Features
Kingdom	Animalia	Common limpets belong to the animal kingdom because they have many cells, need to eat food, and are formed from a fertilized egg.
Phylum	Mollusca	A common limpet is a mollusk because it has a shell, a muscular foot, and a radula.
Class	Gastropoda	A common limpet is a gastropod because it has a single-valved shell, a head with tentacles, and a well-developed foot used in crawling.
Subclass	Prosobranchia	Common limpets are prosobranchs because they are marine snails with a shell, a mantle cavity, gills, and one pair of tentacles on the head.
Order	Archaeogastropoda	Common limpets belong to this order because they browse on algae and have very strong shells that can be clamped down onto the rocks. They have numerous rows of teeth on the radula and a shiny lining to the shell.
Family	Patellidae	Members of this family have conical, ribbed shells and are found on rocky shores.
Genus	*Patella*	A genus is a group of species that are more closely related to one another than to any other members of a family. *Patella* is the genus for the common limpet.
Species	*vulgata*	A species is a group of individuals that can interbreed successfully. *Patella vulgata* is the complete name for the common limpet.

Mollusk Evolution

About 35,000 fossil mollusk species have been identified and described. Mollusk fossils are found in sedimentary, or layered, rocks, such as limestone, chalk, and clay. Fossilized shells are common in the limestone used for buildings, and it is also possible to find shells and impressions of shells in exposed rocks on mountains and cliffs.

Mollusks first appeared about 580 million years ago, and by 500 million years ago, gastropods, bivalves, and cephalopods had evolved and existed in great numbers. Mollusks were common in most marine ecosystems. The next major event in the history of mollusk evolution occurred about 400 million years ago, when some of the bivalves became adapted to life in freshwater. The first land snails appeared 350 million years ago, when green plants began to grow across large areas of Earth's surface.

The fossil record shows that a great number of different mollusk types evolved but many became extinct millions of years ago. It is not possible to trace direct relationships between the living groups of mollusks or to determine a common ancestor with any certainty.

▲ For 125 million years, ammonites were the dominant marine animals. They became extinct 100 million years ago. With their flat spiral shells, there is a resemblance to some present-day mollusks.

▼ The coiled shell of the snail evolved in response to the increase in the size of the body.

present-day mollusks

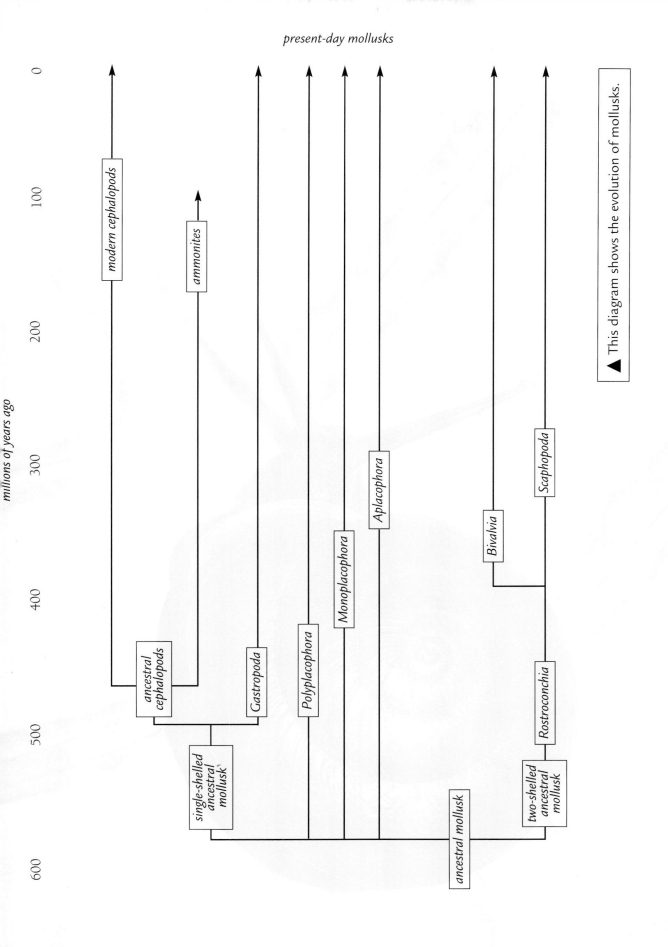

millions of years ago

▲ This diagram shows the evolution of mollusks.

Glossary

adapt change in order to cope with the environment

ancestor individual from which an animal is descended

appendage outgrowth of the body used for feeding or movement

aquatic living in water

arthropod member of the phylum Arthropoda, such as an insect or spider, with jointed appendages and a segmented body

bivalve mollusk with a shell in two parts

browser mollusk that feeds on plant material

buoyancy ability to float

camouflage colors and patterns that let an animal blend in with its surroundings

carnivore animal that eats other animals

cephalopod mollusk with sucker-bearing tentacles or arms

characteristic feature or quality of an animal, such as having a shell or radula

cilia tiny, hair-like structures found on the gills of mollusks. They beat rhythmically, setting up currents and moving mucus.

coral small sea animal that catches food by using its stinging tentacles. Coral live in large colonies called coral reefs.

crustacean arthropod that has antennae, eyes on stalks, and a shieldlike covering over the head and thorax

ecosystem community of organisms and their interaction with the environment

estivation period of inactivity in hot or dry weather

evolution slow process of change in living organisms so that they can adapt to their environment

evolve change very slowly over a long period of time

extinct no longer in existence; permanently disappeared or died out

fertilize coming together of an egg (from a female) and sperm (from a male) to form a new individual

food chain organisms linked together because they depend on each other for food. For example, a plant may be eaten by a slug, which in turn is eaten by a bird.

fossil preserved remains of an organism that lived millions of years ago

gastropod class of mollusks with a broad foot and a single shell

gill organ used to obtain oxygen from water for use in vital body processes

grazer mollusk that feeds on plant material

herbivore animal that eats plants

hermaphrodite animal that has both male and female sex organs

host living organism whose body provides food for a parasite

interbreed mate with another animal of the same species

intertidal zone area on a shore that lies between the highest and lowest points reached by the tides

invertebrate animal that does not have a backbone

larva (plural: **larvae**) young animal that looks different from the adult and changes shape as it develops

ligament tough band of tissue that connects bones or supports muscles

lung body organ through which oxygen is absorbed from the air

mantle outer fold of skin lining a mollusk's mantle cavity that covers the hump containing the body organs and produces the shell if there is one

mantle cavity in mollusks, a cavity, or space, between the mantle and the rest of the body. In aquatic mollusks, this cavity is filled with water and contains the gills.

mate join with a member of the opposite sex so that male sex cells (sperm) can fertilize female sex cells (eggs) in order to produce new individuals

membrane thin sheet of body tissue

mollusk invertebrate that usually has a head, a muscular foot, and an external shell

mucus sticky fluid produced by animals. It moistens and protects body organs.

omnivore animal that eats both plants and animals

operculum cover used to seal a gastropod's shell when the animal has withdrawn inside

organism individual plant or animal

parasite organism that spends part or all of its life obtaining food and shelter from another organism's body

predator animal that catches and kills other animals for food

prey animal that is caught and killed by other animals for food

primitive at an early stage of development or evolution. For example, chitons are more primitive than gastropods.

radula (plural: **radulae**) thin sheet of body tissue covered with rows of teeth

sea anemone animal with a cup-shaped body and a ring of tentacles around the mouth. It attaches itself to rocks.

siphon tube used for drawing in or emptying out liquid

species group of individuals that share many characteristics and can interbreed to produce offspring

streamlined shaped to allow smooth movement through water or air

tentacle in gastropods, a small sense organ attached to the head; in cephalopods, the front part of the foot that has suckers and is used to catch prey

tropical relating to the tropics, the hot regions of the world that lie between the tropic of Cancer and the tropic of Capricorn

venom poison

vertebrate animal with a backbone

Further Information

Fullick, Ann. *Ecosystems & Environment*. Chicago: Heinemann Library, 2000.

Ofinoski, Stephen A. *Snails and Other Mollusks*. Chicago: World Book, 2002.

Sachidhanandam, Uma. *Threatened Habitats*. Chicago: Raintree, 2004.

Townsend, John. *Incredible Mollusks*. Chicago: Raintree, 2005.

Index